TIM MILLER

VROOM!

MOTORING INTO THE WILD WORLD OF RACING

TIM MILLER

Tundra Books

Published in Canada by Tundra Books,
75 Sherbourne Street, Toronto, Ontario M5A 2P9

Published in the United States by Tundra Books of Northern
New York, P.O. Box 1030, Plattsburgh, New York 12901

Library of Congress Control Number: 2005910623

Library and Archives Canada Cataloguing in Publication

Miller, Timothy, 1951-
   Vroom! : motoring into the wild world of racing / Tim Miller.

ISBN-13: 978-0-88776-755-5
ISBN-10: 0-88776-755-9

1. Automobile racing — Juvenile literature.   2. Karting — Juvenile
literature.   I. Title.

GV1029.13.M54 2006   j796.72   C2005-907311-X

ONTARIO ARTS COUNCIL
CONSEIL DES ARTS DE L'ONTARIO

We acknowledge the financial support of the Government of Canada
through the Book Publishing Industry Development Program
(BPIDP) and that of the Government of Ontario through the
Ontario Media Development Corporation's Ontario Book Initiative.

We further acknowledge the support of the Canada Council for the
Arts and the Ontario Arts Council for our publishing program.

Printed in China

1 2 3 4 5 6   11 10 09 08 07 06

*This book is dedicated to my father, John Miller.
Not only did he instill a love and appreciation
of cars and auto racing in me from a very early age,
but he also taught me to follow my dreams.
Thanks, Pop.*

Acknowledgments

I have written for many years, but I want to thank Carolyn Jackson at Tundra for helping me compose a manuscript for the younger, eager mind. I also want to thank Tundra publisher, Kathy Lowinger, for her belief in me and this project.

Thanks also go out to all the photographers who assisted in this venture, but my hat goes off to Rob Potter and Dave Franks. These two photographers, both of whom I have known for a long time, have snapped many a race car over the years, and their dedication and professionalism has no equal.

And to Margie, my wife and best friend, a grade-school teacher whose experiences helped me get inside the minds of young readers, many thanks.

Before we start. . .

Auto racing is a sport of numbers and measurements. How fast does that car go? What size engine does it have? How much fuel does it use? In North American racing, most of these speeds, sizes, and amounts are measured in miles per hour, cubic inches, and gallons, while the rest of world uses metric measurements — kilometers per hour, cubic centimeters, and liters. That's why you will find both imperial and metric measurements in this book.

You can convert the measurements if you like. Here are the basic conversions:

1 mile	=	1.6 kilometers
1 cubic inch	=	16.3 cubic centimeters
1 gallon	=	3.78 liters (liquid)
61 cubic inches	=	1 liter (capacity)
1 pound	=	0.454 kilograms

So, an oval track used by stock cars that was built one mile in length, is 1.6 kilometers long on the metric scale. A five-liter engine is also about 300 cubic inches in size. And if a Top Fuel Dragster burns four gallons of fuel in its quarter-mile race, that is equal to 15.12 liters of fuel on the metric scale.

CONTENTS

CHAPTER

(1)

IN THE BEGINNING

Drivers racing these front-engined roadsters in the 1930s navigated the unpaved tracks through dust and dirt with virtually no safety equipment to protect them.

Almost as soon as cars were invented, the urge to race them set fire to people's imaginations. At first, racing was only a hobby for very wealthy people. Ordinary folks couldn't afford the newfangled machines. Back then, in the 1890s, racing contests were called "tours" or "runs," and the buggies, which had very small engines, had to travel over rough, mostly unpaved public roads. Whoever managed to make it from point A to point B first would receive handshakes from the other drivers and, just maybe, some sort of trophy.

By 1910, though, cars such as Henry Ford's Model T became less expensive and middle- and lower-income families started to enjoy motoring — and racing.

In Europe and Great Britain, roads had been paved almost as soon as cars had appeared. Races were held on those public roads, with all their twists and turns and hills. On race day, the streets would be lined with non-paying spectators who were as close to the action — and sometimes the accidents — as you could get.

In North America, though, there were only dirt and mud trails between many towns and cities. Paved roads didn't appear in any great number until the 1920s. But there were lots of ready-made places to race, as long as the four-legged runners were safely in their stables.

Almost every county fairground had a horse racing track and it was on these dirt ovals that weekend auto races took off. Eventually, many auto-only tracks sprang up, and between 1910 and 1930, tracks made of wooden boards were all the rage. But these were tough to keep in good repair, as the boards broke and splintered because of the weather.

A big change came in 1909, when the Indianapolis Motor Speedway was built in Indiana. Paved with bricks, the huge 2.5-mile-long oval became the top racing spot in the United States; the world famous Indy 500 contest continues there to this day. Known as the "Brickyard" because of its surface, the track is now paved with asphalt, like most highways, but there is still a small section of brick paving left in place for tradition's sake.

By the mid-1920s racing was more organized and very popular on both sides of the Atlantic Ocean. The first circuit built specifically for car racing had been opened at Brooklands, in Great Britain, back in 1906. Europe was already developing a Grand Prix circuit, with many nations building road courses especially for auto racing. This guaranteed more safety for the spectators and meant that the organizers could charge the fans admission to watch races. Italy's famous Monza circuit opened in 1921. France opened the Le Mans course in 1921.

Meanwhile, American tracks, except for Indy and some board ovals, continued to be mostly dirt. But things changed radically in the mid-1940s. Many servicemen returning home from Europe after World War II had seen European-style road racing, and they loved it. Interest in the sport grew and led to the birth of courses such as Watkins Glen in New York and Sebring in Florida.

A group in Daytona Beach, Florida was beginning to organize races with stock North American cars — cars that

YOU COULD RUN AS FAST! Billed as the Race of the Century, an auto race was held in 1895 between Chicago and Evanston, Illinois, a distance of about 54 miles. The winning car took over ten hours to finish the race! That's about five miles per hour.

This pair of Top Fuel Dragsters is at full throttle — that's 12,000 horsepower, or the power in about sixty regular street cars.

anyone could buy from any car lot. Today, stock car racing is the most popular type of racing in North America.

Meanwhile, in Southern California, racers were developing something called drag racing, which pitted two cars against each other down a straight track. Road rallying also began to have a following in America. In these contests, many different sizes of cars travel public roads in a race against time.

The most international type of racing is the land speed trial, where men and speed machines compete to set new records on land. For years these were held on the miles of Florida's hard-packed sand beaches, but as cars became faster and beaches too short, racers started to make their attempts on the vast salt flats of Utah, near the town of Bonneville.

Just about every type of vehicle with four wheels has been customized for racing. And thanks to the pioneers of the sport, many of the technological advances they developed for racing are now regular features in the ordinary cars we drive today.

Getting Down to Basics

We all know that a race is a contest of speed, usually driving some distance with other racers, but it also can be driving by yourself against a time limit.

Most races are run from start to finish, but there are some that are run in many shorter races, called heats, or stages. A heat is usually run over the same track as the main race, but it is shorter, or may not have as many laps around the track. A stage is a short section of a longer course, and several stages are combined to make a whole event.

An organizing body, also known as a sanctioning body, sets the rules for a race, including the specifications of the cars and the tracks, so that the contest is fair for everyone. Auto racing is now one of the most popular of all spectator sports, and is one of the most commercial. Many companies and businesses sponsor the sport and the drivers.

What's So Special About a Race Car?

You may think a race car has more horsepower, bigger tires, or a fancy paint job, and you'd be right. But the *real* difference can be summed up in one word: performance.

A race car, no matter what type, has been developed and changed (or modified, as racers say) from headlights to taillights. Each part of the car has been worked on with one thing in mind: to make it go faster so it can win races.

The engine's power and the car's weight are crucial things. The more power a car has, the faster it will go. In many cases, racing engines are designed, developed, and built for racing only. They could never be used in a regular street car. But a race car's weight is also very important. Here's how it works.

Think of two regular street cars, one red and the other blue. Both cars have 150-horsepower

The steering wheel of this Ferrari Formula 1 car has lots of buttons, dials, and even a small video screen. No horn, though!

FOOD'S ON!

Long ago, when a horse race was held at a fairground, the town ladies would cook up a big meal to take to the track. They would wave their checkered tablecloths at the racers to tell them it was time to stop racing and start eating. The tradition led to the checkered flag that tells drivers the race is over.

engines. But the red car weighs only about 1,500 pounds, while the blue car weighs about 2,000 pounds. With the same engine power but less weight to move, the red car will go faster. Not only will the red car go faster, it will also *perform* better because there is less stress and strain on the tires, brakes, and suspension parts. This means the red car will get up to speed more quickly, go around corners faster, and stop quicker than the blue car.

Race car designers have come up with many ways to make cars light. Some cars, such as those used in Formula 1 or Sprint Car racing, have no fenders, no roofs, and no windows. Stock cars, which do look like cars you see on the street, may have full bodies, but they are made of fiberglass or carbon fiber, materials that are much lighter than what is used for regular cars. And if the race car has any windows, they are made from a type of plastic that weighs less than the regular safety glass in ordinary cars.

Race cars have only one seat and they have absolutely no extras like CD players or air conditioning. Race cars have no mufflers, no windshield wipers, and no spare tire. There's nothing extra that will add weight to slow them down.

Charging Up!

Engines power race cars, just like any other kind of car. Almost all race cars have internal combustion engines that use fuel (like gasoline) and air to produce power. Internal combustion means the actual energy produced — the power — comes from inside the engine and the fuel is exploded (or combusted) by a spark plug.

Though engines come in many shapes and sizes, several basic things determine their power. Perhaps the most important is the size, or "displacement," of the engine. This is determined by the number and size of the cylinders. Cylinders are tube-like parts in the engine. Pistons move up and down inside the cylinders, producing power. The larger the cylinder, the more power produced.

Early auto engines had only one-cylinder engines. But automakers soon realized they could produce engines with more cylinders, so the single-cylinder engine was replaced by two-, four-, six-, right up to sixteen-cylinder engines.

The size of the area in the cylinders determines the displacement or size of the engine. In North America, this measurement is given in cubic inches. In the rest of the world, cubic centimeters are used. Obviously, the larger this number, the bigger the engine.

Engines called V-type have their cylinders in pairs with equal numbers on each side of the engine. Today, many street cars have V6 engines, which are six-cylinder engines shaped in a "V" with two rows, or banks, of three cylinders each.

In racing, several types of multi-cylinder engines are used, and the size, or displacement, of these engines changes with the type of racing. For example, a NASCAR stock car uses a V8 engine of 358 cubic inches, while a Formula 1 engine is a V10 engine of 1.5 liters, or 1500 cubic centimeters.

Here's an early dirt track car from the 1920s racing on a county fairgrounds track where horses usually raced. That wooden fence wouldn't be much help to the fans in the infield if a car crashed through.

An Extra Boost

Racers are always looking for ways to beat the competition. There are many devices used on racing engines, but perhaps the two most common are the turbocharger and the supercharger. Both help "charge" the engine for more power.

Turbocharger – This is a compressor that increases power output by boosting the oxygen entering the engine. Waste exhaust gasses (like those from the tailpipe of your street car) are pushed through a fan, called a turbine, which in turn helps push the fuel through the engine for more power. A turbocharger is simple and lightweight. Several makes of high-performance street cars use this device, and it is quite common on certain race cars, such as those in the Indy Racing League.

Supercharger – A supercharger is a pump that pushes air into the engine's cylinders and is powered by a drive belt from the crankshaft. Also called "blowers," superchargers provide a big boost in the engine's power for short periods of time. They

Today's modern F1 car is quite a different beast, with its large tires, aerodynamic body, and its engine behind the driver. Safety measures are more advanced too, for both drivers and fans.

are not practical for street cars, but they are used in many classes of drag racing where the cars only race for seconds.

Fuel Induction – For many years most regular car engines used a device called the carburetor. It converted the fuel and air into a fine mist that ignited in the engine. Now most street and racing cars use a fuel injection system to force fuel through small nozzles under pressure in precise measured amounts. Also known as an FI system, fuel injection is much more efficient and easier to maintain than a carburetor. Carburetors are still used in racing, mostly stock car racing such as NASCAR.

Racing Talk

Now that you understand a bit about the cars, here are some standard terms that are used throughout the racing world. These will give you a better understanding of auto racing.

Lap: one complete drive around a race track.

Qualifying, Lap Times, and Heat Races: Just as in other sports, you must first qualify for a race. Say there is a race where only thirty cars are allowed to compete. If fifty cars show up to race, only the thirty fastest are allowed in the race. There are several ways to qualify. You can drive on the course as fast as you can against the clock. The less time it takes you, the better starting spot you will get in the field of thirty cars. If yours is the tenth-fastest time, you will start in the tenth position. But if thirty other drivers have turned in qualifying times faster than yours, you won't get to start the main race.

The other main way drivers qualify in a big race is to run in a series of races, called heats, with less laps than the main race. The top two or three finishers in each heat will make up the starting field for the big event, called the feature. This method of qualifying is usually used in Oval Track racing.

Oval Track: This is the basic shape of the track for many types of racing, such as Indy car and stock car racing. The cars drive along a straight section, called a straight (naturally!), turn left into corner one, keep turning left through corner two, and then they're on the other side of the track on another straight section. Then it's back to another left turn, this time corner three, and then corner four, and then they're back on the straight section where they started. (No, drivers don't get dizzy going round and round because the straight sections are long, but you can see why these tracks are called "roundy-rounds.")

Circuit: This term is usually used for a road course track, which has both left and right turns, long straights, short straights, and hills.

Horsepower: You will be seeing the word "horsepower" a lot in this book. We all know that more horsepower in a car's engine makes it go faster, but what actually *is* horsepower? Well, it's a term of measurement, but to understand it you have to know what a foot-pound is. A foot-pound is moving one pound of anything one foot. Sounds simple, right? But to get just *one* horsepower, you have to move something as heavy as a big semi-truck one foot. Power that can pull 33,000 foot-pounds

SHAKE IT UP!
We know the strength of an earthquake is measured on the Richter scale. If a quake hits five on the scale, then there is damage to houses and property. A Top Fuel Dragster or Funny Car under acceleration can hit two on that scale. So it's no joke that these cars are called "ground-pounders."

per minute is one horsepower, because that's what the normal horse can pull. So if you have a car with 100 horsepower, it's almost like having 100 horses in your car. And each horse has enough power to move a semi-truck!

Now you're ready to learn some of the basic types of auto racing:

A group of Formula cars, colorful single-seaters, dive into a corner in an amateur, or "club," race.

Single-seater Racing: Popular all over the world, this is perhaps the best-known form of auto racing. The cars are built specifically for racing, and could never be driven on the street. They are also known as open-wheeled cars, because there are no fenders. The cars often have aerofoil wings in the front and rear to produce "downforce." Downforce is the force of the air that rushes around the speeding car, pushing it down so the car stays closer to the ground. It helps the tires stick to the track.

Most single-seater racing works on a system of levels, just like other sports. For oval track cars, you start off in small, slower cars — karts or Quarter-midgets — and work up to the next level of faster cars, such as Midgets or Sprint cars, to the top classes, which are the Indy-style cars.

The same applies to single-seater road racing cars. But here we have the "Formula" system, where you start off in kart, progress to Formula Vee or Formula Ford cars, then work up to Formula Atlantic cars. When you reach the top, or major league of racing, you are in Formula 1, also called Grand Prix, cars.

Stock Car Racing: In this kind of racing the cars look very similar to the ones you see on the street. But anything that isn't absolutely essential is removed, like the seats and the glass and the spare tire. Then the cars are fitted with crash protection to keep the driver safer. They are driven on oval tracks of pavement or dirt. These cars are very popular in North America, and thousands of fans follow NASCAR, the world's richest stock car racing series.

Road Racing: Road racing cars, or sports cars, may look like some cars on the street, but they are often stripped down and highly modified like stock cars. These racing cars compete on road circuits. They also take part in endurance, or long-distance events, such as the Le Mans 24-hour race in France, or the 12-hour race at Sebring in Florida. These cars are in a race to see how many laps they can make in the time allowed. The racers who travel the farthest in the time length, like 12 or 24 hours, are the winners. These types of races are popular all over the world.

Drag Racing: A drag race is a contest between two cars. Whoever goes the fastest, wins. The cars line up together and from a standing start, they accelerate over a measured distance, either a quarter-mile or an eighth-mile. You race against only one car. If you win, you go to the next round with another racer. The losing driver of each round is eliminated. If you continue to win until there are no more competitors, then you have won the race. This may sound simple, but there is a lot more to drag racing, as you'll see in the section devoted to it.

Rallying: Any kind of car can be used in rally racing, from regular street cars right up to cars that have been highly

Rallying is the one form of motor sport that goes on no matter what the weather. Drivers have to race through whatever they encounter on the route — even ice and snow.

specialized specifically for rallying. Rallies are held on public roads, usually in remote areas of the countryside, where the roads can be closed off to regular traffic. The rally is conducted over a series of stages, or separate sections. The rally team has a driver and a co-driver, or navigator. They are allowed to check out the course before the race so that they know what they will be facing. The navigator has notes on how to drive through the stages, and as the team is racing, he tells the driver what to expect — a sharp corner, mud, a steep hill to climb, or a stream to cross.

Competition in rallying is usually based on time through the stages, and the fastest time wins the stage.

Other Types of Racing: There are several other types of racing, but they all use the same basic rules and methods. And the goal is the same: to go the fastest and win the race.

In **Off-road Racing**, various types of specially modified vehicles, such as pickup trucks and Volkswagen-powered dune buggies, race along off-road areas that no regular street car would be able to handle. Most of the time there are no real roads, just paths through the sand and dried-up creek beds.

The most famous off-road races are the Baja 1000, which is held in the deserts of western Mexico, and the Dakar Rally, which starts from European cities such as Paris, France or Lisbon, Portugal, and goes all the way south into Northern Africa to the city of Dakar, Senegal.

Monster Truck Racing is also very popular, especially in the United States. The trucks sit very high off the ground with their huge earthmover tires and 1500-horsepower engines. Two Monster trucks line up, each one in front of a row of wrecked cars. They must drive over these obstacles in the quickest time to beat their opponent. These trucks usually compete indoors and at county fairs.

So how do race drivers—and racing fans—stay safe? Well, the truth is that sometimes they don't, but safety is one of the sport's most important concerns. It is also one of the things that has changed the most over the years. Standard items today, such as seat belts and helmets, weren't even considered in the early years of racing.

Before World War II, racers wore only leather hats and goggles. These protected drivers from flying dirt and stones, but not much else. And as far as belts went, drivers felt that their chances of surviving a crash were better if they were thrown out of the car rather than being stuck inside it. Cars had no rollover bars, so drivers were often pinned under flipped cars. Fuel tanks exploded on impact, causing hideous burns and injuries.

Eventually, even the most daring of drivers could see the sense in safety measures. At first, they used simple lap belts and better helmets. These have evolved into the aviation-style five-point harnesses and full headgear we see today. Drivers' suits are now made of fire-retardant material, something no one even dreamed of in the early days.

Cars became safer too. Special fuel cells were developed to stay in one piece, even on impact. Roll bars became compulsory, and tires were designed to reduce blowouts at high speeds. Full-bodied, full-fendered cars, such as stock cars and endurance road racing cars, now have nets on the driver's side window so that the arms are kept inside in case of a rollover.

DRIVER SAFETY

Drivers are now protected from head to toe before they even buckle up inside a car. Since the head is the most vulnerable part of the body, the helmet is key. These days, helmets are made from very strong materials such as carbon fiber or Kevlar. They are designed to lessen the force of impact and keep the head from being bounced around. A layer of foam inside helps absorb shock and keep the head steady. Most helmets have face shields of tough but flexible plastic to protect the eyes and face.

FASTEN YOUR SEATBELT!

In addition, most drivers now use a piece of equipment called the HANS (Head and Neck Support) device. A type of collar attached to the helmet, it was developed by an engineer and a racer, and keeps the head from snapping forward or sideways in a crash.

Drivers also wear fire-retardant suits, special shoes, socks, gloves, and head coverings (called balaclavas) under their helmets. The fire-retardant material gives them about 40 seconds of protection if there is a fire—just enough time to escape if they are lucky.

SPECTATOR SAFETY

You can imagine the scene if a car roaring around a track at top speed blew a tire, lost control, and flew into a crowd of fans. This nightmare actually happened in France during the 1955 Le Mans endurance race. A Mercedes-Benz, going at about 150 miles per hour, hit a slower Austin Healey and hurtled end over end into the jam-packed grandstands. It was the worst crash in motor racing history—eighty-two people died.

It used to be that bales of hay or old tires were all that kept out-of-control cars from the crowds. Track workers, called marshals, were stationed along the circuit to try to keep fans away from the track. These days, metal barriers like those on public highways protect the fans. The courses also have "run-off" areas at the end of a long straight section of the track. Drivers can head for these to stop safely if their brakes fail. Other areas off the track are filled with gravel to slow down any runaway cars. And finally, many circuits around the world have installed energy-absorbing walls—a kind of big cushion around the track. Instead of smashing into concrete walls, the car bounces into the pad, which is usually filled with some kind of foam. This not only stops the car, but it also softens the impact and protects the driver.

Everyone involved with racing knows the risks that are part of the sport, and they put a lot of effort into making it as safe as they can for drivers and their fans.

LET'S HIT THE ROAD

Road racing can be one of two types. True road races are run over actual public roads that have been closed off to the public temporarily. The Formula 1, or Grand Prix race held in the tiny country of Monaco in Europe each year is an example.

The other type is run on tracks built especially for auto racing. These tracks are situated in the countryside, and are built with left- and right-hand corners, hills, and bridges. They are designed to be more like the original road races held on public streets and roads.

In the last couple of decades, temporary road circuits have been set up in city centers for all types of road racing, including Grand Prix, Formula Atlantic, and sports car events. Some familiar temporary courses include Long Beach, California, Miami, Florida, and Toronto, Ontario.

Let's have a look at the most popular forms of road racing.

F1 cars speed along the track during a Montreal Grand Prix race. This is a very expensive form of racing, so teams raise money by charging sponsors to have their company's logo painted on the cars.

Grand Prix Racing

The words "Grand Prix" are French for "great prize" and this racing is the highest level of motor sport in the world. It is second only to soccer in popularity as a world sport, and the cars and drivers of Grand Prix, also called Formula 1 (or F1), are worshipped by millions of fans.

The cars are very high-tech, very expensive, and very fast. While F1 racing used to take place mainly in Europe, the eighteen or nineteen races each year are now also held in North America, Africa, China, Australia, and Malaysia.

F1 races are about 180 miles long and have a two-hour time limit. They are controlled by the Federation International de l'Automobile (FIA), headquartered in Paris, France. About ten teams and twenty drivers and cars compete in each of the weekend events.

The race itself is always held on Sunday, but before that there is a practice day and then the qualifying race. Qualifying is a "flying lap" where a car and driver go as fast as possible. The lower the time, the closer to the front of the pack that driver will be for the real race the next day. The very lowest time goes to the pole position, a term from horse racing where the first racer starts at a pole that marks the start/finish line. (There really is no pole in today's races, but the term is still used.)

The cars start the race from a dead stop at the start/finish line. The drivers keep their eyes glued to five sets of red lights. When all the red lights go off, the race is on!

Now all the drivers are going as fast as they can. And that *is* fast. These cars have powerful ten-cylinder engines and close to 1,000 horsepower, but they are light — only a little over 1,300 pounds. A regular family car weighs about 3,000 pounds and only has about 150 horsepower, so you can see why the F1 car will be a *lot* faster.

The cars can roar up to almost 200 mph on some race circuits. But they pay a price for all this power and speed — fuel consumption. On average a Grand Prix car gets about four miles

Ferrari driver Michael Schumacher has won six Grand Prix titles, more than any other driver. He is a true world champion.

per gallon of gas. Your average family car gets anywhere from five to ten times that distance, even when it is carrying more than one person! So all the drivers must pull into the pit at least once during the race to get more gas and sometimes new tires, too. Pit stops are very important. The faster the pit crew gets the gas in the car, the sooner the car can get back into the race.

When the race is over, the first-, second-, and third-place drivers celebrate on a special stand called a podium. Because Grand Prix racing has teams from all over the world, the national anthem for each of these top three drivers is played.

As soon as the trophies are presented, the fun begins. Each of the three winners is given a huge bottle of champagne. They shake up the bottles and spray each other, the officials, the reporters and photographers, and anyone else who happens to be nearby. Then it's off to the media center where they answer questions about the race.

There are at least 15 crew members working on this F1 car, changing tires, fueling the tank, and making adjustments. Each member has a specified task and works as quickly as possible to get the driver back on the track.

SPEAKING OF MONEY . . . .

OPERATING A GRAND PRIX TEAM is very expensive. The cars are expensive, the drivers' salaries are expensive, and the traveling is expensive. Ferrari has been the top team for many seasons, and has a win-at-all-costs game plan. It seems that money is no object to Ferrari. Let's look at what Ferrari spends to go racing.

It costs the team about $5 million every year to build its cars and all the spare parts they require. This does not include research and development, or wind-tunnel testing. And this does not even include the engines, which are worth about $1.1 million each! Just think how many regular cars you could buy for the cost of one Ferrari engine.

Now you've got to get the cars and the team to the race. At least 60 people from the team travel to each race. And they don't drive to the races, or camp out in tents when they get to the race track. They travel on planes, live in hotels, eat in restaurants, and drive around in rental cars. Getting the team to the race, then housing and feeding them can cost more than $1 million for each race.

But it's not over yet. Ferrari spends close to $2 million to race its cars at each event. That includes paying the team members, which costs more than $200,000 for each race. Then there are the drivers' wages, which start at about $160,000 and go all the way up to more than $2 million for each race.

Most F1 teams have sponsors that help pay a huge chunk of the expenses, usually about 80 to 85 percent. A "title" or main sponsor can spend anywhere from $30 million to $100 million to have its name or logo on the side of the race car. Other money for the team comes from television profits and the actual prize money of the race itself.

In 2004, for instance, Ferrari spent about $426 million on its team. Toyota came next with $397 million, and McLaren Mercedes was third with $359 million. At the other end of this list is one of the "poorer" teams, Minardi-Cosworth. That team only spent about $40 million to race in 2004. You can see that to race a two-car F1 team it would help to own a bank or two!

This may seem like a very glamorous life, but it is also a very hard life, both physically and mentally. Grand Prix drivers must be in superb shape, have excellent coordination, and be mentally focused while racing. And for nine months of the year, a driver travels around the world to all the races. In fact, between actual racing and lots of car testing, a Grand Prix team travels about 160,000 miles a year. That's like traveling all the way around the world more than six times and it doesn't leave much time to spend at home.

What does a Formula 1 car have in common with the car you drive to the mall? Four wheels, and that's about it!

Today's F1 car is the ultimate in racing technology. Everything about an F1 car is built for speed and handling. In fact, you wouldn't want to drive it to the mall. Yes, you could get there fast, maybe with a speeding ticket as your trophy, but the F1 car has no lights. It has no windshield wipers. And it has only one seat.

Here are the facts:

The F1 car is a single-seat, open-cockpit (no roof), open-wheeled (no fenders) racer. It is powered by a 3.0-liter, ten-cylinder engine with no turbocharger or supercharger. While the engine size is equal to or a little smaller than most mid- to large-size cars you see every day on the streets, the F1 engine develops about 900 horsepower. That's about six times more power than the family car can work up! And this engine can run at 19,000 revolutions per minute (rpm). The engine in the family car would blow up at anything higher than 6,000 rpm.

Most F1 cars have a six- or seven-speed transmission that is shifted electronically by special flappers, or paddles, on the steering wheel. The driver does not use the clutch pedal, he just flicks the paddle one way to upshift and go faster, or back the other way to slow down to go around corners.

And an F1 car is certainly not shaped like the two- and four-door sedans you see on the roads. As with airplanes, the sleek F1 shape has been developed to offer as little wind resistance as possible so it can go faster. F1 cars also rely on other aerodynamic features such as large wings. Air pushes down on these wings when the car is at speed, which helps keep the car stable and gives the tires better traction.

Speaking of traction, an F1 car uses special race-only tires made of a rubber that is much softer than the rubber used for regular car tires. These soft tires provide more grip on the racing surface and better traction through the corners. But they last only a couple of hundred miles. Tires on the family car can be used for at least 30,000 miles.

THE F1 CAR

Race drivers are well-paid. Most of them earn millions of dollars in a season. Even drivers on the lower-budget teams earn about $3 million a year — about $160,000 per race. Michael Schumacher, a driver for the Ferrari Team, was the highest-paid athlete in the world in 2004. He made about $2 million for each race. That's more than $36 million a year. Pretty good money for a Sunday afternoon drive!

Sports Car Racing

Almost everyone knows and loves sports cars. We see them on the streets every day. Most are small, two-seater cars, often convertibles, with manual transmissions, performance engines, and stiff suspensions to offer better performance and road-holding.

These cars are racing in the American Le Mans Series. The front car is a racing-only Prototype-class car, while the yellow car in the center is a highly modified Chevrolet Corvette that competes in the Grand Touring class.

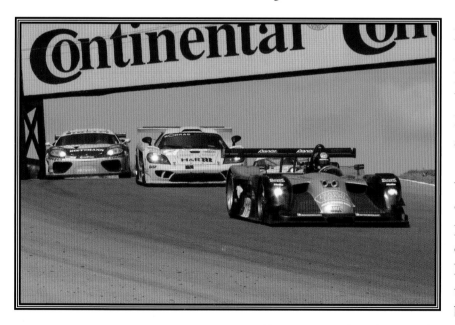

At one time there were lots of British sports cars, such as the MG, Austin-Healey, and Jaguar XKE, but today we see more Porsches, Mazda RX7s, and Chevrolet Corvettes.

Years ago, owners would drive their sports cars to the race track, park in the pit area, strap on a helmet, cover their headlights with masking tape so they wouldn't break, and pull up to the start line to race. After the race, those drivers would head home, and the sports cars they had driven in a race on Sunday were the same cars they drove to work on Monday.

Today, the top sports car events are for professional race teams with big budgets and a large team of drivers, mechanics, and support staff. Most of the events in these Endurance and

Prototype contests are races of long distances — 600 miles or more — where endurance is the key to winning. The cars are usually driven by a team of two or three drivers who switch every couple of hours.

The cars themselves are regular sports cars, but are highly modified with high-performance engines, tires, and bodywork. They have lights, so they can be driven at night, and radios, so the driver can talk with the crew members back in the pits.

Along with the cars you would recognize from the street, such as Corvettes, BMWs, and Mustangs, there are special classes for "prototype" cars. These are based on regular production cars, but are out-and-out racing machines equipped with whatever new technology the car company is developing. They are usually open-cockpit cars with swoopy bodies and big engines, and feature lots of things that eventually may end up in regular cars. Car manufacturers often test and modify new developments for brakes, safety equipment, and engines on racing prototypes before they appear in regular cars.

Sports car racing takes place all over the globe. Some of the more famous races include the 24 Hours of Le Mans in France and the 24 Hours of Daytona in Florida. As the names tell you, these races last the whole day.

Here's a regional or club race of sports cars that features modified street cars such as BMW, Porsche, and Toyota, but the car in front is a Cobra, developed in the early 1960s. It has a British-built body with a large-horsepower, American V8 engine.

The Weekend Racer

Another kind of sports car racing, "regional" or "club" contests, takes place at circuits all over North America. Cars entered in these races come from the local region, or from a "club," a group of drivers/owners of a certain type of car, such as the BMW club, or the Porsche club.

Many classes of cars race against each other in these contests and they are matched up in the fairest way possible — according to the size of their engines. All the big-engined cars such as Jaguars, Corvettes, and Mustangs race against each other, while Toyotas will race against BMWs and Alfa Romeos.

Open-wheeled, or Formula cars, race at these events too, on an amateur level. These cars resemble their big brother F1 cars, but have much smaller engines. They are also much cheaper to race. Here you'll see classes such as Formula Ford, which race with 1600-cubic centimeter, four-cylinder Ford engines, or Formula Vee, a class that is based on the old-style Volkswagen Beetle engine and suspension.

Touring Car Racing

This form of racing is very popular in Europe and Australia, and is similar to stock car racing in North America. But rather than racing on oval tracks, touring cars compete on road racing circuits. Like stock cars, touring cars are heavily modified versions of cars you would recognize on the street, cars like Mercedes-Benz, Audi, and Honda.

Touring car teams start with a standard two- or four-door sedan bodyshell, but just about everything else is changed for racing, including engines, brakes, tires, and suspensions. The cars also feature lots of wind and air foils to help their handling at high speeds, and are equipped with full roll cages and other devices to protect the driver.

Fans can relate to these cars because they look like the cars they see on the street, and because they are not terribly expensive to build and race. They are very popular with both the drivers and fans, and are fun to watch.

Trans-Am

This is one of the longest-running series, and cars in the Trans-American Sedan Championship are the closest looking to cars you see on the streets. They race on tracks throughout Canada and the United States.

When the Sports Car Club of America (SCCA) first started the series in 1966, there were two classes in Trans-Am: cars with under two-liter engines, such as Porsche, BMW, and Alfa Romeo; and cars with over two-liter engines, which were mostly small American cars such as the Ford Mustang, Chevrolet

NIGHT LIGHTS
Most race cars don't have lights. But some race at night during long events like the 24 Hours of Le Mans, and they have lights over the numbers on their sides so that the scoring officials can keep track of their progress.

Camaro, and Plymouth Barracuda. The larger cars were limited to a five-liter (302-cubic-inch) engine size.

The years between 1967 and 1970 were dominated by driver Mark Donahue, driving a Camaro and an AMC Javelin. This was the height of Trans-Am racing's popularity, as fans could relate to the cars. They could go to a car dealership and buy almost the same car for themselves to drive on the street.

By 1980, the cars were becoming more and more sophisticated as the rules changed, and the stock-appearing cars were replaced with out-and-out racing machines.

Trans-Am racing continues to be popular and exciting with Chevrolet Corvettes, Ford Mustangs, Dodge Vipers, and Jaguar XKRs in tight, wheel-to-wheel, fender-banging action on road courses, temporary street courses, and airport courses.

DRIVING ON THE EDGE

Rally cars are driven all over the road to maintain their speed, but usually stay very close to the drainage ditches at the edge of the road whenever they can. When going around corners with ditches, the driver will hang the front wheel right at the edge of the ditch to keep up his speed. This is known as "ditch-hooking."

Rally Racing

A rally is really just a car meeting. But it doesn't involve sitting around and exchanging opinions, although a rally can be very noisy. Instead, the cars take to the roads in one of two main types of contest — either in a navigational rally or a performance rally.

A rally car is built not only for speed, but it must also be tough enough to handle landing after jumps such as this.

Navigational Rally

In a navigational rally, cars and teams run over public roads, just like we all do when going for a drive in the country. But these cars are competing against each other in time, speed, and distance.

A driver and a navigator, who tells the driver where to go, take their car over a special route set out by the

organizers, usually on little-used roads in the countryside, although there are times when the cars must drive through towns and built-up areas. The team must get from point A to point B in a specified time. There are official stops along the way, called checkpoints. The teams have to stay within the speed limit, because if they go too fast and arrive early at a checkpoint, they lose points. As in most other sports, the team with the most points wins.

Performance Rally

This type of rallying involves driving as fast as you can along country roads. The team with the lowest time wins. A performance rally is held on roads that are closed to regular traffic, and the roads are usually unpaved. The cars in this type of rally are highly modified, and the driver and navigator have many years' experience at this level.

These races are held all over the globe, and in extremes of climate, from the torrid desert heat of the Middle East to the frigid cold of Scandinavia. Most of these events, such as the ones organized by the World Rally Championship, are held in many separate stages — some have as many as twenty-seven. All of the events are more than 620 miles long. While drivers and navigators get some well-earned sleep, team mechanics work on the cars overnight.

In any type of rallying, teamwork is important. The team takes notes about the course, or each stage, before they begin, and these notes are used by the navigator to tell the driver what to expect on the road — where the curves are, where the road narrows, when they are coming to a stream they have to cross or a mountain they have to climb.

CARS IN THE AIR
Cars are not supposed to fly, but if you get going really fast over a bump, the car becomes airborne, which is okay for a few seconds. In rallying, a car will go as fast as it can at the end of the timed stage, quite often on a section of bumpy road, so it could be in the air at the end. Rally people call this "the flying finish."

CHAPTER 3

ROUND THE OVAL TRACKS

All types of cars race on oval tracks, which are very common in North America, and which developed from horse racing. Quite often, eighty or ninety years ago, a track would race horses one day and cars the next. Sometimes, when auto racing was still new, promoters raced horses and cars together. And many times the horse would win because the car would break down. As cars got faster and more reliable, however, horses were no match for the machines.

While there are many types of oval track cars, they fall into two basic kinds: open-wheeled cars and full-fendered, or full-bodied, cars. A car that races at the Indianapolis Motor Speedway is an open-wheeled car and has no fenders. A car that races in NASCAR is a full-fendered car. The NASCAR vehicles are also known as stock cars because when this type of racing got started, the cars were basically "stock"—driven right off a car lot and onto the race track.

Close, colorful, and exciting are three of the best words to describe NASCAR Cup stock car racing. Here the cars are four wide at the Talladega Speedway in Alabama.

LET'S HOPE HE HAS A BIG WALLET!

In 1959, a ticket to see the first Daytona 500 cost $8. Lee Petty won the race and took home $19,050. In 2005, the same seat cost $120 and the winner of the race, Jeff Gordon, stuffed almost $1.5 million in his wallet.

Both types of car have loyal fans. Open-wheeled fans say real race cars don't have doors. Stock car fans point out that even the slightest contact between two open-wheeled cars usually leads to an accident.

Both types of cars have their strong and weak points. Open-wheeled cars are lighter and nimbler, while stock cars can push and shove each other around with little or no damage to either the car or the driver.

As well as two types of cars, oval track racing has two kinds of tracks. They can be paved, usually with asphalt, just like the street you live on, or they can be dirt tracks (because this type of racing started on horse racing tracks, remember?). But not just any kind of dirt. Most dirt tracks are made of clay. Either type of car can race on either type of track.

There are many sizes of oval tracks, from quarter-mile "bull rings" to the large 2.66-mile Talladega Speedway. Most tracks have banked, or sloped corners, so that the cars can go faster around the bends.

Now let's look at the classes of cars that race on oval tracks.

Indy or Champ Cars

The top class in oval track open-wheeled racing is the Indy, or Champ car class. These are the fastest and most powerful of the oval-track cars, and are raced mainly in North America. The cars are given these names because they are the kind of cars that raced at the Indianapolis Speedway (nicknamed the "Indy"), and the Championship Trail many years ago.

Today, these cars race in two series, CART (Championship Auto Racing Teams) and the IRL (Indy Racing League). CART is also known as the Champ Car World Series.

Whether it's CART or IRL, the cars have their roots in the open-wheeled, front-engined vehicles that raced on dirt, pavement, and board tracks.

While not quite as powerful or fast as F1 cars, Champ and Indy cars have closely followed F1 advances and technology.

Today's cars are highly sophisticated machines that can race on oval tracks, road courses, and temporary street courses at speeds of more than 230 mph. This versatility has made them popular.

This is probably the most dangerous form of auto racing. Since the cars have no fenders, when one car races down a track close to another, their wheels can lock together, usually resulting in extensive damage. Luckily, the drivers are highly skilled professionals who take no chances. They act and react with quick reflexes to almost any situation on the track.

With their wide tires made of very soft, sticky rubber and their sophisticated suspensions that can be adjusted by the driver while he is racing, these cars can dart around other racers with a speed and agility that make fans gasp in amazement.

The IRL series takes place mostly on oval tracks that are at least two miles long, like the Indianapolis Motor Speedway and the Michigan International Speedway, where they can really show off. There are a couple of IRL road circuits — Watkins Glen in New York and California's Infineon Raceway — and there is one race in Japan.

It's hard to believe, but these modern Indy Cars (or Champ cars) have evolved from the dirt track racers of the 1920s and 1930s. Similar to F1 cars, but not quite as sophisticated, the Indy cars race on both road courses and oval tracks.

The CART cars compete on ovals such as the Milwaukee Mile, and in Las Vegas, but they also race on temporary street circuits in Toronto, Long Beach, and Cleveland. The series is truly international in scope, with events in the United States, Canada, Australia, South Korea, and Mexico.

Other Open-wheeled Racers

Sprint Cars

The popular open-wheeled Sprint car is a very simple racing machine. It has roots going back decades, and without any modern safety equipment, it looks very similar to dirt track cars of the 1930s.

Sprint Cars are powerful and crude. With large V8 engines and a car weight of 1,500 pounds, a Sprint Car has a power-to-weight ratio of an F1 car. There is no excess weight on a Sprint Car. If you don't need it to race, it's not there. No extra body work, no transmission, no clutch, not even a starter. Trucks push the cars to get them underway for a race. The rear tires, especially the right one, are very large and are made of a soft rubber compound to help keep them on the track during all the left-turn corners.

There aren't any comforts for the driver in a Sprint Car either. The driver sits over the rear axle with his hands on a steering wheel that is almost flat, like the steering wheel on a city bus.

Sprint Car races are very fast and very exciting, as the cars dart around the track with the right rear tire scrabbling on the surface for traction. The cars are always throwing up chunks of the clay track. One driver may keep down low on the track, and another may ride way up near the edge. Both are looking for the fastest "line" around the track.

Sprint Cars are often evenly matched, and they are usually bunched up in tight formation from the start,

Sprint Cars have roots dating back to the 1920s and have not changed too much since then, except that today they have wide tires, big engines, and wings on top to provide better handling. They go very fast around a dirt oval track.

SPRINT CAR MATH

HERE'S SOME MATH FOR YOU. Let's say you're driving a Sprint Car on a half-mile track, and you average 120 mph per lap. That means you're driving a half-mile, which is a couple of city blocks long, in 15 seconds! It would take only 30 seconds to drive one mile. Now let's say in your family car, you are driving at just under the speed limit at 60 mph. The family sedan will take an hour to get you 60 miles down the road. A Sprint Car will get you there in 30 minutes! You'd have time for a hamburger and a shake while you waited for the sedan to catch up.

which makes for exciting, hold-your-breath racing. The races are very short. Even the features, or main events, are no more than thirty laps. The cars are well named, and they "sprint" to the finish.

One unique feature of a Sprint Car is the wing it carries on top of the driver's roll cage. The adjustable wing provides downforce to help the car stay on the track.

Most Sprint Car races are run on short dirt tracks. When everything is going well, a car can average 120 mph for a lap and get up to at least 130 mph on straight sections.

Sprint Car racing is popular in North America, New Zealand, and Australia.

Midget Cars

These cars started out as smaller, scaled-down versions of the Indy "Champ" cars of the 1930s. The cars were small enough that they could race on temporary tracks set up in football stadiums. Midgets are reasonably affordable and are raced all over North America. There are two main versions of the car and both types look very similar. They weigh about 1,100 pounds, have 13-inch wheels, and a short wheelbase of about 75 inches. One version uses motorcycle engines and the other type uses a stock Ford Focus engine with about 135 horsepower. Both types race on dirt and paved tracks.

Although a Midget is small, it is capable of high speeds. A regular Honda Civic, for instance, has a wheelbase of 103 inches, weighs more than twice as much as a Midget, and has an engine of only 115 horsepower. You can see that the Midget could outperform the Civic.

Quarter Midgets

If you think Midgets are small, then take a look at a Quarter Midget, which is about four times smaller than a Midget. Quarter Midgets, like karts, are a great way for young people to start racing. There are lots of racing clubs for youngsters from five to sixteen years of age. The cars, rules, and safety procedures are designed specifically for young racers, and events are held on short oval tracks of about 1/20th of a mile.

Safety features on these cars include a full roll cage, seat harness, and full face gear. This racing class can boast of fewer competitor injuries than little league football.

The car itself has a tubular frame and fiberglass body. Two engines are used, a 2.5 horsepower and a 4-horsepower engine just like the one that's powering the lawnmower you push around the yard every weekend.

Quarter Midget racing is a family-oriented sport that teaches safe driving skills that can be applied later on when you are old enough to get the keys to the family car.

Modifieds

This class of cars has been around since World War II, and the term "modified" originally meant modified stock car. The car was essentially a regular street car, but had a roll cage and high-performance engine.

During the 1960s and 1970s, these cars changed a great deal. The older coupe bodies were getting very hard to find in auto-wrecking yards, so racers started using the bodies of smaller, more modern cars such as the Chevrolet Vega, Ford Pinto, and AMC Gremlin. Gremlin bodies were boxy and flat, and racers could build these bodies at home rather than buy a wrecked car and strip it.

In the early 1970s, a race car builder named Dick Tobias began to build a complete Modified car with the chassis, body, and suspension components. So now racers didn't have to hunt

WELL-OILED

Years ago, if you had an upset stomach, your mother might give you a spoonful of castor oil. It's a thick, clear, horrible-tasting oil that comes from the castor bean plant. But Midget race cars love it. The thick oil keeps engine parts lubricated and when it's hot, it smells a lot better than regular engine oil.

around for parts and build their own cars. All they had to do was buy one of these kit-type cars, put in an engine, paint the body, and head for a track.

Today's Modifieds have gone through major suspension, brake, and axle (also known as running gear) changes, especially the cars that are driven on dirt ovals.

These cars are very popular in the northeastern U.S., and in Ontario and Quebec in Canada. They race in three classes, depending on engine size. While not as fast on a dirt oval as Sprint Cars, they are exciting to watch as they tilt way over on their suspensions powering through the corners.

Specialized Open-wheeled Racers

There are many other open-wheeled racing machines that compete on oval tracks, both pavement and dirt. Here's a list of some of the more popular classes.

Silver Crown Cars – These cars look similar to Sprint Cars, but are longer, have no wings, and race only on asphalt tracks up to a mile in length.

Super Modifieds – These are the fastest cars in the world on a paved short track under a mile in length. They are the ultimate in power and handling where money is no object. With large wings for better track grip and big engines of 850 horsepower, Super Modifieds race like Sprint Cars, but on asphalt. They are very popular with fans.

Vintage Modifieds – There are several racing groups in North America that race these cars, which resemble the old "jalopy" racers of the 1940s. They have old car bodies, but are right up to date in the safety, suspension, and engine departments.

TQ Midgets – The TQ Midget, is another downsized Midget racer. The TQ stands for three-quarters. A full-size Midget has a wheelbase of 76 inches, and a TQ Midget has a wheelbase of about 60 inches. The cars weigh 650 to

TEAR-OFFS
Drivers who race on dirt ovals have dust and dirt flying all round them, and there are no windows to protect them. Drivers have a face shield, but it gets dirty too. Instead of wiping it off, the driver has disposable clear sheets on the front of the shield. When one gets dirty, the driver rips it off and has a clear view. The sheets are called tear-offs and on a mucky day, a driver can go through thirty of them in a hundred-lap race.

They may be small at just 650 pounds and with 125 horsepower engines, but Three-quarter Midgets are very fast and nimble and provide lots of excitement.

900 pounds, and use motorcycle engines. They have fat wheels and tires, and with wings on the rollcage, look like baby Super Modifieds.

Stock Car Racing

Stock car racing — in its many forms — is the most common form of auto racing in North America. There are more than 1,000 oval tracks in the North America, both asphalt and dirt, and stock cars race on almost all of them.

The cars in this class were once actually the very same cars you see on the street. There are many level-entry classes for what are basically street cars with the glass, interior, and exhaust system removed, and a roll cage added. They're not very fast and they don't handle very well, but they are entertaining and a good learning ground for faster divisions of cars. Stock car racing is also the cheapest way to go racing.

As in other sports, you start off as a novice, or learner, and as you get better and your skills become stronger, you move up to the next level. You race at the small local tracks each week, and if you're good enough and have enough money, you can start to compete in faster, more advanced cars and eventually move up to professional stock car racing, like the NASCAR Cup circuit.

We're going to focus on the top class in stock car racing, the NASCAR Cup.

In close NASCAR Cup stock car races like this, the make of car may be difficult to tell, but fans know their hero drivers by the large number on the car's door.

NASCAR Cup Racing

This series has exploded over the last few years. NASCAR (which stands for the National Association for Stock Car Auto Racing) started in 1948, mostly in the southern U.S. The series featured the Modified division, which consisted of old coupes with high-performance engines, and the Strictly Stock division, where cars could be taken right out of the dealer showroom and raced.

But by the mid-1950s these Strictly Stock cars were becoming less "stock" and more "modified," built especially for racing on the small dirt oval tracks. Some automakers supplied high-performance engine and suspension parts, and drivers such as Curtis Turner, Tim Flock, and Lee Petty became folk heroes driving their Plymouths, Chryslers, Fords, and Oldsmobiles.

In 1959 NASCAR founder, Bill France, took a big step and built the 2.5-mile Daytona speedway in Florida, where the cars reached new speeds on the paved track.

During the 1960s more large paved tracks were built, and the old traditional dirt ovals fell by the wayside. The sport grew in popularity and professionalism, and corporate sponsors started to appear. Carmakers built cars specifically to win races. Tire companies devoted people and money to developing special racing tires.

In 1971 NASCAR entered what is considered its modern era, when large companies began to put money into NASCAR races and teams. They believed they would sell more of their products when the crowds could see the company name on the side of a car or on the banners advertising a race.

There was little television coverage in the early years, but the Daytona 500 was broadcast live in 1979, and since then NASCAR races have been a feature on national television. They are as popular as baseball and football games. Today's NASCAR world is one of excitement, color, and lots of money as teams spend millions of dollars a year to win the Nextel Cup, the prize of a series of thirty-six races held all over the United States.

NASCAR Drivers

NASCAR Cup drivers are some of the best-known names in sport. Fans learn all about

THAT'S A CROWD
One NASCAR Nextel Cup race draws more fans than a Super Bowl, World Series, and NBA finals game combined.

The cockpit and dashboard of a NASCAR stock car is all business with lots of gauges and switches. No air-conditioning, windshield wiper, or CD player in these cars!

NASCAR vehicles are covered with the sponsor and product logos of companies that help pay for the racing. And they're not all related to autos. This car has logos of a grocery store chain, a sports drink, and a video game company on its front fender.

their favorite driver's life, and often stand in line at races to get his autograph. They wear hats and shirts with their favorite drivers on them, and put stickers showing their favorite drivers on the back of their own cars or trucks.

NASCAR drivers are treated like movie or rock music stars. They are well-paid, but they spend most of their time each year away from home, either racing, testing, or taking part in promotional appearances. Some drivers have won more than $60 million.

NASCAR drivers work long and hard hours to get to the top of stock car racing. They are true professional athletes.

The NASCAR Car

Today's NASCAR Cup car is an out-and-out racing machine that is anything but "stock."

Each part of the car is specially designed, built, and tested. The cars used today are the Chevrolet Monte Carlo, Ford Taurus, and Dodge Charger, but they have very little in common with the street-driven, front-wheel drive, V6-powered sedans that you can buy at a dealership.

Basically, a Cup car is a rear-wheel drive, V8-powered car with a body based on a U.S.-made, full-size passenger sedan. The frame is manufactured of round and square tubing. The roll cage is an important part of the frame. There are three elements to the car body: the front clip; the driver's compartment; and the rear clip. The front and rear clips, which are the front and rear ends of the car, are collapsible and are supposed to crush in an accident to help cushion the driver from the impact, just as helmets and shoulder, knee, and elbow pads do for football and hockey players. This is an important safety feature that now is used in many of today's regular cars.

The engines in NASCAR Cup cars are of V8 design, and limited to 358 cubic inches. They run on gasoline like you can get at the local filling station, but this gas is of the high-test variety. The engine also uses a carburetor, which mixes the gas and air that goes into the engine. A NASCAR engine produces 750 to 800 horsepower, runs at 8,000 rpm for long periods of time, and costs at least $40,000.

NASCAR Cup cars are very tough, and will take a lot of punishment. You will see the cars touching and bumping into each other. This is just part of the excitement. NASCAR Cup cars are built like tanks and are very safe. In almost every case when a car is involved in a bad crash or rollover, the driver is protected and will walk away from the crash.

These are not sleek cars. There are small air spoilers at the front and rear, but there are no big wings or air scoops like on Formula 1 and Indy-type cars. Even so, the cars can obtain speeds of over 190 mph on the larger tracks.

NASCAR Races and Tracks

NASCAR holds Cup races on oval tracks in thirty-six events each season. Two of the races are on road courses. No matter where the cars race, the procedure is the same. The teams perform some testing to get the cars "dialed-in" or performing exactly the way they want them. Then the cars go on the track one at a time and go as fast as they can for two laps to qualify for the main race.

There are forty-three starting positions for each race. If fifty-five cars show up to qualify, you have to get a time that is at least the forty-third lowest to get in the big race. The lower the qualifying time, the better position the driver gets at the start of the race.

Depending on the track, the cars can race up to 500 miles, which is like driving from New York City to Buffalo, or from Toronto to Chicago. But these cars travel at an average speed of 160 to 170 mph, a lot faster than highway speeds of 65 mph.

On the day of the race the cars are lined up in their qualifying order, and after a couple of pace laps where the car's engines and tires are warmed up, an official waves the green flag to start the race.

IT'S THE REAL THING
One of the best examples of NASCAR's popularity is shown in this statistic provided by Coca-Cola. In 2000 the company sponsored the National Basketball Association and produced vending machine graphics featuring popular NBA players. Coke received 254 orders for these machines. The next year Coke featured NASCAR Cup drivers on the vending machines. Orders came in for 55,000 machines!

In a NASCAR pit stop only seven crew members are allowed to work on a car, so this team must work even faster than an F1 team to get the car back in the race. The long pole is used to clean the debris away from the front of the car. The two team members at the rear are fueling the car, the member to the right is working the jack, and the other four are putting on new tires. All this is done in about 18 seconds. How's that for service?

Then for the next few hours the cars go as fast as they can for as long as they can. There are usually caution periods — when a car has hit the wall, or there has been a collision, or there is some debris on the track that could pose a problem. When a yellow, or caution, flag is waved, the cars must maintain their position and not do any passing.

When a caution flag does come out, most cars will scurry into the pits for more fuel and a tire change. This is a very important aspect of a NASCAR race. When the cars come in to the pit for servicing, a team of seven members goes into action. One person jacks up the car and four others, working in pairs, change each tire, one at a time, while the remaining two manually fill the fuel tank.

What may look like a disorganized group of people tripping over each other, is in fact a highly skilled operation that they have practiced for hours and hours, so that they can get the car serviced and back out to the race as quickly as possible. Many races can be won or lost in the pits.

RACING FLAGS

Green: Used at the beginning of a race, and for restarts. As with a green light on city streets, the green flag means the way is clear and racing may proceed.

Red: There is a danger on the track, and cars must stop as quickly as possible. This flag is used if there is a serious crash, the track is blocked, or weather conditions are poor.

Yellow: Known as the caution flag, this is used where officials decide the track is not clear. The yellow flag may be displayed for an accident, debris on the track, or poor weather. In most cases, cars must maintain their positions, passing is not allowed, and laps are counted.

Blue/Yellow stripe: This is an information flag, and is waved at a driver about to be overtaken by a faster car. The slower car must move over to allow faster competitors to overtake.

Black: The black flag is displayed to a driver when a mechanical problem or a rules infraction is noted by officials. A car must enter the pits when black-flagged.

White: Signifies there is one lap remaining in the race.

Checkered: Waved at the end of the race when the scheduled distance has been completed.

While most sports work up to a season-ending big game, like the Super Bowl in football or the World Series final in baseball, NASCAR starts right away with its biggest event. The Daytona 500, considered the sport's top race, kicks off the NASCAR season each February.

After the Daytona 500, the teams race almost every Sunday until the end of November. They race on a variety of track sizes, from the half-mile ovals at Bristol, Tennessee and Martinsville, Virginia to the 2.5-mile super speedway of Daytona and the biggest track on the circuit, the 2.66 mile oval at Talladega, Alabama. There are also a couple of races on road courses, at Watkins Glen in New York State, which is 2.45 miles long, and California's Infineon Raceway, which is almost 2 miles long.

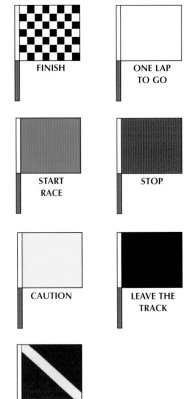

FINISH

ONE LAP
TO GO

START
RACE

STOP

CAUTION

LEAVE THE
TRACK

MOVE TO
OUTSIDE

Most of the tracks' stands feature private suites and boxes, just like football and baseball stadiums, lots of food concessions, and a manufacturers' midway, where companies show and demonstrate their auto-related products for the fans.

Speaking of fans, NASCAR does pack 'em in. North Carolina Speedway, also known as Rockingham, has permanent seating for 60,000 people and it is considered small. The Brickyard 400 at Indianapolis Motor Speedway has seats for 250,000 fans! Average attendance for NASCAR races is over 100,000, which is a lot more than for any football or baseball game.

Other Stock Car Series

While NASCAR Cup racing is the big gun of stock car racing, there are many other stock car series that have lots of fans and plenty of good racing. Most are stepping stones to making the grade at the NASCAR level, just like racing a kart is the first step for anyone who wants to become a Grand Prix driver.

In fact, NASCAR has several smaller series under its name. There is the Dodge Weekly Series, held at many tracks across North America, and the NASCAR Regional Racing Series, also held across the continent featuring a variety of race cars. The Craftsman Truck Series is next in the NASCAR chain, then the Busch Series. Once you're good enough to race in the Busch Series, you are ready for the NASCAR Nextel Cup.

But there are other stepping stones to NASCAR Cup racing. Most of these series are regional. The Automobile Racing Club of America, for instance, holds about twenty events per year in the eastern half of the United States; the American Speed Association series is based in the Midwest.

The Canadian Association for Stock Car Racing holds events across Canada and the American Canadian Tour operates races in the northeastern U.S. and Quebec and Ontario. The United Speed Alliance Racing group hold events mainly in the southern U.S.

No matter where these races are held, they are almost all run on short tracks. This is gritty, heads-up racing, with lots of pushing and shoving, and almost all NASCAR Cup drivers have graduated from this type of oval track racing. In fact, several Cup drivers sometimes make special appearances on these small tracks when their schedules permit.

Almost every oval track has at least one division of stock car racing on an amateur level. The cars race on dirt or paved tracks. There are several types of classes. Here's a rundown on some of the more popular ones you can see at your local track each week:

Mini-stocks – These are the smallest stock cars. Almost all are compact cars with four-cylinder engines — Hondas, Ford Mustangs, and Toyotas.

Street Stock – These cars are V8-powered older Chevrolet Camaros, Monte Carlos, Dodge Chargers, and similar cars with no engine changes, street tires, and a roll cage.

Here's a scene that takes place hundreds of times each weekend all over North America. This is local track stock car racing, also called short-track racing because the ovals are usually less than half a mile in length.

NO HOT AIR HERE

When you pump up your bike tires or top up the tire pressure in the family car, that's regular air you are using. But most race car tires are filled with a gas called nitrogen, which helps the tire pressure stay the same during the race.

Late Model – A step up from the Street Stock cars, Late Models are true race cars with high-performance engines, suspensions, and racing tires.

Legends Cars – These are scaled-down Ford and Chevrolet bodied-cars from the 1930s and 1940s that resemble the old NASCAR Modifieds. They are powered by 122-horsepower motorcycle engines. Legends cars have become very popular with drivers and fans, and are a great way for a young driver to get into the racing world.

Super Late Models – This is the fastest class of fendered race car you will probably see at your local track. They have few restrictions on engine size and power, and have wild-looking bodies to cut down on wind resistance. Cars must resemble a domestic auto, such as a Chevrolet Monte Carlo or Camaro, or Ford Thunderbird.

Jeff the Karter

Karting is a great way to get into auto racing. You can get behind the wheel and enter an organized event even if you're only five. It's safe, teaches you great coordination skills, and best of all, it's lots of fun.

Jeff May lives in Mount Hope, Ontario, and has been racing karts since he was five. He started in an old kart with a small engine, and has worked up to his present kart, which is powered by a 15-horsepower engine.

That may not sound so powerful, but Jeff's kart only weighs 300 pounds, so he can race along at speeds a lot faster than your parents can drive on the streets.

Jeff and his dad, Randy May, work together as a family team. Randy works on the car and Jeff races. Jeff's dad also raced karts when he was Jeff's age, and thought Jeff would like to try racing.

"I started driving karts when my dad got me an old Honda and I would drive it around on Grandpa's back lawn," says Jeff. The racing bug bit Jeff hard, and it wasn't long before he left the backyard far behind.

"Jeff picked up on it quickly," explains his father. "And when he started going through Grandma's rock gardens, I knew it was time to get him on the track."

Jeff's progress has been steady, and he has had several victories in about 100 races over the years. Aside from his driving skills, he has learned to be an important part of the team, and he can tell his dad how the kart is performing on the track.

"He's very methodical on the track," says his father, "telling me how the car is, so when he comes in I can make the proper adjustments."

Racing a kart isn't as inexpensive as many other sports. The kart Jeff drives is worth about $4,000.

Jeff also fits soccer and hockey into his busy schedule. And while karting is important to him, and is a family activity, Jeff doesn't forget his schooling. His dad says, "If the marks drop, the race car goes."

Jeff would like to race bigger cars when he gets older. His dad races a Three-quarter Midget car. "I'm ready to try the bigger car any time," states Jeff. "And I would probably do better than Dad at racing it," he adds, grinning.

CHAPTER

(4)

IT'S A DRAG!

Once considered the "bad boy" of auto racing, drag racing has become one of the most popular forms of the sport, and it is certainly the simplest. This is a contest that relies on excellent hand-eye coordination and on having the quickest car. There are no laps, no corners, and no pit stops. When you pull up to the starting line, you have to be ready — there's no second chance.

Two cars line up at the end of a long, straight section of track, usually a quarter-mile long. The drivers watch the lights on a timing device known as a Christmas Tree, and when the green light goes on, they pound down on the gas pedal. Whoever gets to the end of the track first is the winner, and goes on to race again. The loser gets to park his or her car.

These contests started in Southern California in the late 1940s, where illegal races were staged on public roads, usually at night, away from built-up areas. But the police got wise to the racers in their souped-up coupes and roadsters. Eventually, with cooperation from racing organizations and police, drag races began to be held legally on old airport runways.

You'll have no problem believing that this is one of the fastest-accelerating cars on the planet. It's a Top Fuel Dragster, and with at least 6,000 horsepower, a Top Fueler can speed up to 300 mph in less than five seconds from a standing start.

At first, there were no clocking systems to tell the drivers how fast they were going, or to decide on a winner. But eventually clocks, triggered by breaking a beam of light, were developed, and today these timing systems are good for one one-thousandth of a second.

During the 1950s, drag racing grew at "strips" all across North America. The sport became very specialized, and cars were built in a variety of classes just for racing. These cars ranged from everyday family sedans to out-and-out speed machines designed and built only for one thing — to go as fast as possible.

There are more than 300 drag racing tracks in North America. The sport is also popular in some European countries, such as Britain and Sweden.

Here's a look at some drag racing classes.

PLUG YOUR EARS!
All race cars are noisy, but nothing is as loud as a Top Fuel Dragster. Roaring down the drag strip it can reach a decibel level of 175. (A decibel is a measurement of noise.) That's only five decibels less that the noise of a rocket launching! Ear protection is very important.

Top Fuel

This is the fastest class in drag racing. In fact, Top Fuel cars are the quickest-accelerating cars on the planet. Today's Top Fuel car can go from 0 to about 330 mph in under five seconds. That's like sitting at a stop light, and, when the light turns green, getting up to that speed in the space of about three city blocks.

Top Fuel cars are powered by engines that produce about 6,500 horsepower from a 500-cubic-inch, aluminum V8 engine. And with a weight of about 2,200 pounds, these rear-engined cars will go from 0 to 60 mph in just one second!

But there is a trade-off for all this speed. The cars run on an exotic and expensive fuel called nitromethane, and up to sixteen gallons of it are burned for each race. The engine is so finely tuned that it must be stripped down after each race and checked over. Any parts that don't meet the strictest requirements must be replaced, so you can

This Top Fuel Dragster is ready to take off. The flames are coming from the nitromethane fuel that is burned in the engine. The high wing helps stabilize the car at high speed.

RACERS AS ATHLETES

You might think anybody could race a car. You just sit in a car, step on the gas, and steer, right?

Well, those might be the basics, but you have to be better at working the pedals and turning the steering wheel than the rest of the racers on the track if you want to win. Not only must you have excellent hand-eye coordination, but you also have to be cool, calm, and collected. You have to think fast and concentrate fully for every second of the race. You have to predict and judge what is coming around every turn. You need to be mentally tough.

Racing is also strenuous physically, but not in the same way as football, hockey, or soccer, where there is contact with other players. In auto racing, your body becomes a part of the car. In some ways it is like riding a horse, where you and the horse are working together to achieve a goal.

Good professional race car drivers have to be in top physical shape to maintain an edge over the other racers. Normally the heart pumps between 60 to 100 times a minute. During a race, the driver's heart is pumping at about 150 to 200 beats per minute. That's as much as the heart of a marathon runner or a long-distance cyclist would beat during a race.

As well, when drivers go round corners, they have to be able to stand a 4.5 lateral g-force (g-force is the gravitational pull of Earth on your body, like when you ride a roller coaster. But lateral g-force is from side-to-side rather than up and down like on a roller coaster). In simple terms, this is like going around a corner on your bike with a 50-pound weight attached to your head.

Not only that, a driver's body temperature can rise four or five degrees in a race because of the heat, vibration, and gravitational pulls on the body. If you have a temperature of two or three degrees above normal, that usually means you are pretty sick. So you can see that although a race driver doesn't run or tackle or skate, he must be in top condition to withstand the strains put on his body.

see that racing a Top Fuel car is very expensive. Even if the race car is paid for, the crew works for free, and nothing blows up during a race, it still would cost about $1,000 *per second* to race.

Early Top Fuel cars were called Rails or Rail Jobs because there was no body on the cars and the engine sat in the frame rails in front of the driver. Today's Top Fuel car has the engine in the rear, behind the driver. The move was made to protect the driver in case the engine blew up while racing down the track, which often happened. Also, since the engines are tall, the driver could not see very well when they were in the front.

In 1971, drag racing pioneer Don Garlits, known as Big Daddy, suffered some serious injuries when his Top Fuel car blew up. The car broke in half, and after Garlits recovered, he designed and built the rear-engined dragster that we see today.

Presently the fastest Top Fuel speed is 335.57 mph, and the fastest time is 4.42 seconds.

Funny Cars

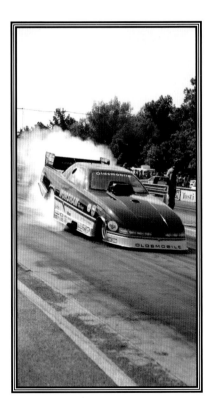

A Funny Car produces lots of noise, smoke, and action. They are very popular with the fans.

They may have a weird name, but these cars are not funny to drive. Running the same powerful engines as the Top Fuel class, these popular cars have carbon fiber bodies on a very short frame, with a wheelbase only half as long as a Top Fuel car. With such a short car, and all that power, it takes a lot of work to keep a Funny Car going straight down the race track.

Also known as Floppers, because the one-piece body flips up from the front so the driver can get inside the car, Funny Cars were developed in the late 1960s as exhibition cars. They had standard car bodies, but sat on frames longer than normal, with the wheel wells near the front and rear ends of the car, making the car look "funny."

But the fans loved these cars, and eventually they became a class in drag racing. Today's Funny Cars offer more excitement and noise than any other type of race car. They are louder than what you would hear standing beside a jet airplane, and under full acceleration they can literally shake the ground.

THE CHRISTMAS TREE

DRAG RACING IS THE ONLY type of major motor sport that does not use the traditional flags for controlling a race. It uses an electronic device called a Christmas Tree because of its shape and all the different colored lights on it.

Two light beams cross the starting line area, and these are wired to the Tree and electronic timers. When the car's front tires break the first light beam, the car is "pre-staged." Then the car moves ahead a few inches to break the next light beam, and the car is now "staged" or ready to race.

When both cars are staged, the starting official clicks a switch and the lights on the Tree start to come on. The large yellow lights below the staging lights blink one after the other. Then the green light comes on, and it's time to go! But if you're anxious, and you start before the last yellow light goes off, then the red light at the bottom comes on, and you're out of the race.

If the drag race between the cars is in a Pro category, such as Top Fuel, Funny Car, or Pro Modified, all three large yellow bulbs light at once, and then the green lights up. For Sportsman class cars, each one of the three yellow lights shines one after the other, with half a second between each light. So you can see you have to focus on those lights — you can't be daydreaming, because that guy in the next lane could be half way down the track before you get going!

Other types of racing use a flagman to start races, but the electronic timers in the Christmas tree work in thousandths of a second, faster than any human can.

Funny Cars are not quite as fast as Top Fuelers, because they weigh more and they aren't as aerodynamic. The speed and time record set in 2004 by John Force of California, with a time of 4.665 seconds and a speed of 333.58 mph, was unbroken in 2005.

As you can imagine, driver safety is crucial in a car that's going this fast. There is a trap door in the roof in case the driver must get out in an emergency. Drivers wear more fire-proof clothing than in other classes, and there are three on-board fire extinguishing systems in the car.

Pro Modified

Although quite new to drag racing, the Pro Mod division has become very popular with fans. These cars capture the true spirit of drag racing's roots, and are the ultimate hot rods.

Powered by supercharged or nitrous-oxide powered engines of over 500 cubic inches, Pro Mods run the quarter-mile in the 6.20-second range at up to 230 mph.

This class now offers different body styles that are very exciting. Cars range from old 1933 Willys coupes or 1949 Mercurys to modern-looking Corvettes. These cars, with their fully-enclosed bodies, are called the world's fastest doorslammers.

The Pro Modified cars are known as doorslammers because the driver must use a regular car door to get in and out. A relatively new class, Pro Mod racing is very popular.

Pro Stock

Another official professional category in drag racing is Pro Stock. These are modern, full-bodied cars that look very similar to cars you see on the street. But don't let their appearance fool you. These are dedicated racing machines capable of 6.60-second quarter-miles at just over 200 mph.

Body styles in Pro Stock include cars such as the Pontiac Grand Am, Ford Escort, and Dodge Stratus. In order to keep a stock-looking appearance, just about the only modifications that are allowed are a small rear spoiler and large air scoop on the hood.

Unlike other Pro classes, Pro Stock cars must run on gasoline, just like regular street cars. There are no superchargers on a Pro Stock car. The gas goes through a pair of large carburetors. While this may seem like backward technology, a good Pro Stock V8 engine of 500 cubic inches can produce 1,350 horse-power at more than 10,000 rpm. Attached to this powerful engine is a five-speed racing transmission, which the driver must shift as quickly as possible.

While a Pro Stock car may show many changes underneath to make it go fast, the headlights and taillights must remain in their original place, and the cars must weigh at least 2,350 pounds.

Exhibition Cars

Exhibition, or "show" cars in drag racing travel from track to track, much like old carnival or circus performers, and race against each other in special shows called exhibition runs. The cars are some of the wildest creations in all of motor sport. A Wheelstander, for instance, takes off from the start line and within a short distance is running down the track on its rear wheels only. These cars, which offer entertainment for the fans between rounds of regular racing, are very popular, just like the clowns between acts at a circus.

Exhibition cars come in any and every shape and size. There are fire trucks and school buses and ambulances and cars that run backwards, along with regular-looking cars and trucks. These vehicles are as wild as the imagination allows.

The other popular exhibition class is made up of jet-powered vehicles and is considered more main stream than Wheelstanders. Based on the jet engines of military airplanes, jet cars make lots of flames and smoke and are very exciting at night. There are jet-powered dragsters, Funny Cars, and even full-size semi trucks.

Sportsman Classes

Here is where the majority of drag racers compete. The "pro" classes are true "heads-up" racing, where the cars race only against themselves and there are no rules on engines or power. In the Sportsman classes, such as Super Gas, Competition, and Super Stock, cars are "dialed in," which means they make their own times through a series of runs down the track. This special time is called an index.

One car may clock a time of 9.90 seconds while another, more powerful car can go faster, say 7.90 seconds. These two cars are paired up, but they don't start the race together. The slower car gets to start first, while the faster car waits at the starting line. This is all controlled by the electronic timing system and the yellow lights on the Christmas Tree. When the faster car starts, the slower car can already be way down the track. But the faster car may catch up to the slower car. Whoever crosses the finish line first wins the race.

But remember the times the cars "dialed in?" Well, if the slower car goes faster than his set time of 9.90 seconds, such as 9.50 seconds, he loses the race because he has broken out of his "index." He cannot go faster than his pre-set time.

All Sportsman classes offer exciting racing with a wide variety of car types. You may see supercharged dragsters running against older stock-looking station wagons.

This dragster is actually powered by a jet airplane engine. Built for entertaining crowds, jet dragsters offer lots of fire and smoke, and some very high speeds, for the fans.

In the Stock and Super Stock classes, the cars are very restricted to changes. ET Brackets is another form of drag racing, designed to be an affordable way to race. Just strap on a helmet, go through technical inspection, and start racing with your street car. This class also runs on the dial-in system, so driver skill is more important than modifications to the car.

Drag racing is one of the few types of auto racing where you can compete in the car you drive on the street. Just take off the hubcaps, put on the helmet, roll up the window, and get going!

Junior Dragsters

If you're interested in drag racing, but think you're too young, read on.

Starting in 1992, young people were given the chance to compete in drag racing with the introduction of Junior Dragsters.

These cars are half-size dragsters, powered by 5-horsepower engines just like the engine in the family lawnmower, but are built for speed rather than cutting grass. A rear-engined Junior Dragster can take you down the track at speeds up to 85 mph, which is a lot faster than going down Suicide Hill on your skateboard.

Junior Dragster racing is divided into age groups. Drivers 8 and 9 years old may run up to 45 mph for 12.9 seconds. Drivers 10 to 12 years old may run as fast as 8.90 seconds, and drivers 13 to 17 years old may run as fast as 7.90 seconds.

Junior Dragster racing is a great way to start racing. You have to "stage" the car, which means set the car up correctly on the starting line, watch the start light on the Christmas Tree, and keep the car straight in your lane down the track. There are thousands of Junior Dragster racers, driving cars that cost from about $4,000 to more than $15,000. Most drag strips have Junior Dragster programs, and national competitions offer scholarships as part of the prizes. By the time you're ready to drag race in a full-size car, you've got lots of good experience under your belt.

Keely Benner,
Junior Dragster

Keely Benner can't wait for weekends.

That's when she gets into her fire suit, puts on her fireproof shoes and gloves, and goes drag racing.

Keely is one of thousands of young drag racers across North America who compete in the Junior Dragster division. This class offers youngsters from 8 to 17 the basics of drag racing in cars that resemble the mighty Top Fuel class.

Not only is Keely getting a rush driving fast in a controlled environment, she also is having a lot of fun competing and spending time with her family. Keely's dad, Mark Benner, used to race himself, but gave it up a few years ago so he could get Keely behind the wheel. Keely started with a 15-horsepower car that could travel the eighth-mile distance in under 13 seconds. Now her car is powered by an all-out racing engine of 38 horse-power that can get her down the track in less than nine seconds at over 75 mph.

"When I was younger I saw the Junior Dragsters when I went to the track with Mom and Dad," said Keely. "I thought I'd like to do it. It looked cool and like a lot of fun."

With the support and help of not only her immediate family, but her grandparents and other family members, Keely races about fifteen times a year in her little dragster painted black with flames down the sides. She soon started to be called "Little Shirley" after one of her racing heroes, drag racing legend Shirley Muldowney.

"When I got in the faster car I was ready for it and wanted to race it, but I was a little nervous," she said. "But after I made my run, I was really excited, whooping and hollering when I was finished. It was a real adrenaline rush."

As a Junior Dragster veteran, Keely is well aware of the car and its capabilities, and if something isn't quite right, she can explain the problem to her Dad. "She is very good at telling me how the car is," said Mark. "I respect her judgment, and she is usually right."

Keely doesn't win every race, but she does have a wall lined with trophies in her house in Kohler, Ontario. She races against a few girls, but she especially likes to beat the boys. "I can show the boys that girls can win and that they aren't better than us," she says.

Keely and her mom, Marne, explain that good sportsmanship is a big part of racing a Junior Dragster. "There's always a handshake and pleasantries after a race," Marne says. Keely nods in agreement. "We always shake hands after the races, no matter what."

FOR MORE INFORMATION

Check out these Web sites for even more racing information:

FOR FORMULA 1:

The official F1 site – www.formula1.com
Federation Internationale de l'Automobile (FIA) – world
    governing motorsport association, headquartered in Paris,
    France – www.fia.com
F1 facts and data – www.f1db.com
F1 site – www.f1.racing.com
Shell Oil site with lots of Ferrari information –
    www.shell.com/motorsport
Toyota's F1 site – www.toyotaf1.com
Minardi's F1 site – www.minardi.it
Williams/BMW F1 site – www.bmw.williamsf1.com
Jordan's F1 site – www.f1jordan.com
McLaren's F1 site – www.mclaren.com
BAR/Honda F1 site – www.barhondaf1.com
Informative site showing Michelin's involvement in F1 racing –
    www.michelinman.com/motorsports/teams

FOR ROAD RACING:

Sports Car Club of America – www.scca.com
Canadian Automobile Sport Clubs – www.casc.on.ca
International Motor Sports Association – www.imsaracing.com
American Le Mans Series – www.americanlemans.com
Grand American Road Racing Series – www.grandamerican.com
Australian Supercar Touring Sedans – www.v8supercar.com
British Touring Car – www.btccpages.com
FIA World Touring Car – www.eurostc.com
Le Mans – site featuring the famed track – www.lemans.org
Karting Sites: www.worldkarting.com,
    www.canadiankarting.com, www.kartinguk.com

FOR RALLYING:

World Rally Championship – www.wrc.com
U.S. Rally Championship – www.unitedstatesrallychampionship.com
Major rally events – www.worldrally.net

FOR DRAG RACING:
National Hot Rod Association – www.nhra.com
International Hot Rod Association – www.ihra.com
Pro Modified racing – www.promodifiedracing.com
Drag racing general – www.competitionplus.com
Junior dragsters – www.jrdrags.com

FOR STOCK CAR RACING:
National Association for Stock Car Auto Racing –
    www.nascar.com
Canadian Association for Stock Car Auto Racing – www.cascar.ca
Auto Racing Club of America – www.arcaracing.com
United Speed Alliance Racing Pro Cup – www.usarprocup.com
American Canadian Tour – www.acttour.com

FOR OVAL TRACK RACING:
Championship Auto Racing Teams – www.cart.com
Indy Racing League – www.indycar.com
Sprint Cars – Sprint Car Racing Association – www.scra.com
All Star Circuit of Champions – www.allstarsprint.com
United States Auto Club – Midgets, Sprints, Silver Crown –
    www.usacracing.com
Three-quarter (TQ) Midgets – American TQ Midgets –
    www.atqmra.org
Dirt racing – Drivers Independent Race Tracks –
    www.dirtmotorsports.com
International Motor Contest Association – www.imca.com
Super Modifieds – International Super Modified Association –
    www.ismasupers.com
Englewood Racing Association – www.erasupermodifieds.com

GLOSSARY OF RACING TERMS

AERODYNAMICS: As applied to racing, the study of airflow and the forces of resistance and pressure that result from the flow of air over, under and around a moving car.

AIR DAM: The front valance of the vehicle that produces downforce while directing air flow around the car.

ANTI-ROLL BARS: Bars in the front of the car that help control how much the car tips from side to side.

APRON: The paved portion of a race track that separates the racing surface from the (usually unpaved) infield. The very bottom of the race track, below the bottom groove. If a car has a problem, the driver goes there to get out of the way.

BACK STRETCH: The straight on a circle track between turns two and three.

BALANCE: A term to describe downforce, front to rear.

BANKING: The sloping of a race track, particularly at a curve or corner, from the apron to the outside wall.

BLISTER: Excessive heat can make a tire literally blister and shed rubber. Drivers can detect the problem by the resulting vibrations.

BLOCKING: Racing term for changing position on the track to prevent drivers behind from passing.

CHASSIS: The basic structure of a race car to which all other components are attached.

COMBINATIONS: Combinations of engine, gearing, suspension, aerodynamic parts, and wheel and tire settings that teams forecast will work under varying conditions and tracks.

COMPOUND: The rubber blend for tires. In some series, teams can choose their tire compound based on the track and weather conditions. A softer compound tire provides better traction but wears out much faster than a harder compound. Left side tires are considerably softer than right side tires and it's against the rules to run left sides on the right.

DIALED IN: Describes a car that is handling very well. The car isn't loose or tight.

DIRTY AIR: Turbulent air caused by fast-moving cars that can cause a following car to lose control.

DNF: Did not finish.

DNQ: Did not qualify.

DNS: Did not start.

DOWNFORCE: Basically, the downward pressure of the air on a car as it races. Downforce increases with speed. It is determined by such things as front fenders and rear spoilers.

DRAFT: Airflow creates a low-pressure air pocket (or draft) behind moving objects. Most notably in NASCAR, drivers try to follow opponents closely enough to enter their draft. The car creating the draft actually pulls the pursuing driver who can ease off the throttle and save gas.

DRAFTING: Practice of two, or more, cars, while racing, to run nose to tail, almost touching. The lead car, by displacing air in front of it, creates a vacuum between its rear end and the following car's nose.

FEDERATION INTERNATIONALE DE L'AUTOMOBILE (FIA): The governing body for most auto racing around the world.

FLAGMAN: The person standing on the tower above the Start/Finish Line who controls the race with a series of flags.

FOOTPRINT: The amount in square inches that each tire touches the earth. Larger footprints enhance tire grip to track. Four equal footprints with equal applied forces would promote great tire wear and vehicle handling.

FRESH RUBBER: A new set of tires acquired during a pit stop.

FRONT CLIP: The front-most part of the race car, starting with the firewall.

FRONT STRETCH: The straight on a circle track between turns four and one. Also called front straight, or front chute, the start-finish line is usually there.

GOT UNDER: A driver out-brakes an opponent on the inside of a turn and makes a pass.

GRENADED: Destroyed an engine under racing conditions, usually in a dramatic show of smoke and fluids.

GROOVE: The most efficient or quickest way around the track for a particular driver. The high groove takes a car closer to the outside wall for most of a lap. The low groove takes a car closer to the apron than the outside wall. Road racers use the term line.

HANDLING: Generally, a car's performance while racing, qualifying, or practicing.

HEADSOCK: A fire resistant head mask or balaclava.

HOOKED UP: A car that is performing well because all parts are hooked up or working well together.

HORSEPOWER: The estimated power needed to lift 33,000 lbs. one foot per minute roughly equated with a horse's strength.

INSIDE GROOVE OR LINE: On an oval track, this is the inner-most racing line which is usually separated from the infield by a distinctly flat surface called an apron. On road courses, the inside groove refers to the line closest to the curbs.

LAP: One time around a track. Also used as a verb when a driver passes a car and is a full lap ahead of (or has lapped) that opponent.

LAPPED TRAFFIC: Cars that have dropped one or more laps behind the race leader.

LEAD LAP: The race leader's lap

LONG PEDAL: Commonly refers to a car's gas pedal because of the design. Also used to describe a brake pedal when brakes wear out because the driver has to push the pedal harder and further to slow down.

LOOSE: A car has more grip in the front than the rear end and tends to fish tail. Drivers often report whether the car is loose or tight so the crew can make adjustments.

MARBLES: Rocks and debris that collect off the racing line. If a driver enters the marbles at an excessive speed, his car will lose grip.

NEUTRAL: A term drivers use when referring to how their car is handling. When a car is neither loose nor pushing (tight).

ON THE THROTTLE: A driver has the pedal to the metal.

OUT BRAKE: A driver gains time and position on an opponent by applying the brakes later and deeper into a corner.

OVERSTEER: A condition when the front of a car has more grip than the rear. This is the same as a car being loose.

PARADE LAP(S): The warm-up lap before a race. Drivers use this lap to warm up their engines and often zigzag to warm up tires.

PARKING LOT: Term used after a big crash that takes out a lot of cars, making the track look like a parking lot.

PIT STOP: Drivers stop in pit row so their crews can change tires, refuel, and make repairs or other adjustments.

POLE POSITION: The driver qualifying fastest is awarded the first starting position. This means the driver will start on the inside (relative to the first turn) of the first row.

PUSH: The rear end of a car has more grip than the front. This condition makes a car harder to turn into a corner. Commonly known as Understeer.

QUALIFY: During designated sessions, teams must meet established lap times to qualify for (or enter) a race based on the number of spots available.

RACE RUBBER: Race tires as opposed to qualifying tires.

RACER'S TAPE: Heavy duty duct tape used to temporarily repair hanging car body parts that might hinder aerodynamic features and decrease performance.

ROAD COURSE: A race track with multiple left and right hand turns. Generally refers to permanent, purpose-built racing facilities. Can also refer to temporary street courses built on big city streets.

ROLL BAR: Large, sturdy bars designed to protect a driver if the car rolls over.

RUNNING LIGHT: A car running with little fuel. Teams qualify with a light load to achieve maximum speed.

SANDBAGGING: Driver who allegedly fails to drive a car to its full potential in practice or qualifying, thus being able to surprise his or her competitors during a race.

SCRUBBED TIRES: The best kind of racing tire because they've had a few laps of wear to normalize the surface.

SCUFF(S): A tire that has been used at least once and is saved for further racing. A lap or two is enough to scuff it in.

SETUP: The combination of settings for a car's engine, aerodynamic features and tires/wheels. Teams make continual adjustments to a car's setup during pit stops based on driver input.

SHOOT OUT: Two or more drivers race to the end for victory.

SLICK: A track condition where, for a number of reasons, a car's tires do not properly adhere to the surface or get a good bite. A slick race track is not necessarily wet or slippery because of oil, water, etc.

SLINGSHOT: A maneuver in which a car following the leader in a draft suddenly steers around it breaking the vacuum; this provides an extra burst of speed that allows the second car to take the lead. *See Drafting.*

SLIP STREAM: The cavity of low-pressure created by a moving object. In racing, drivers use this slip stream to draft another vehicle.

SPOILER: A metal strip that helps control airflow, downforce, and drag. The front spoiler or air dam is underneath the car's front end near the axle; the rear spoiler is attached to the trunk lid. Adding more spoiler refers to increasing the rear spoiler's angle in relation to the rear window and generally aids a car's cornering ability. Less spoiler (decreasing its angle) aids straightaway speed.

SPOTTER: Crew member at a NASCAR race who is in a building above the grandstands and informs the driver via radio about crashes ahead and traffic coming up behind.

STAGGER: On ovals, teams may use a different size tire (or stagger) on the outside wheel to improve the car's handling ability. The difference in size between the tires on the left and right sides of a car is called the stagger. If the left side tire is 87 inches, and the right side tire is 88 inches, you have one-inch of stagger.

STICKERS: New tire(s). Teams generally use sticker tires during qualifying, then use scrubbed tires in a race.

STOP-AND-GO PENALTY: A penalty which requires a driver to stop at the team's pit for a timed penalty before reentering the race. This penalty can be given for anything from speeding into the pits to contact with an opponent.

TECH: Short for tech (or technical) inspection. Each car is submitted to tech inspection so sanctioning body officials can confirm all chassis and engine parts meet series' guidelines. A "teched" car has passed inspections.

TIGHT: Also known as understeer, the car's front tires don't turn well through the turns because of traction loss. A driver must slow down entering and going through the turns to avoid having the car push all the way into the wall.

TUCK UNDER: A driver follows an opponent close enough to move into (or tuck under) their draft.

UNDERSTEER: When a car has more traction (or grip) in the rear than in the front.

UNLAP: A driver down one lap passes the leader to regain position on the lead lap.

VALANCE: (Also referred to as "front air dam.") This is the panel that extends below the vehicle's front bumper. The relation of the bottom of the valance, or its ground clearance, affects the amount of front downforce the vehicle creates. Lowering the valance creates more front downforce.

WAR WAGON: Or pit wagon. Slang term for the large metal cabinet on wheels that holds equipment in the driver's pit box during the race.

WEAVING: Zigzagging across the track to warm up and clean off tires, or to confuse an opponent while attempting a pass.

WRENCH: Slang for racing mechanic.

Photo Credits

Pages 1, 4, 6	– Author's collection
Pages 3, 41	– Joe Barrett
Pages 7, 14, 26	– Mark Jackson, www.markjackson.ca
Pages 9, 19, 20, 38	– Colour Tech
Pages 10, 22, 51	– Morgan J. Segal
Pages 15, 16, 18, 54-55	– Bridgestone Motorsport
Pages 24, 31, 32, 33, 35, 43, 58	– Dave Franks
Page 27	– Ken Pelkie
Page 30	– Erin Kindred
Pages 40, 50	– Author
Pages 12-13, 42, 44, 45, 46 (top), 48, 49	– Rob Potter
Page 46 (bottom)	– Mike Goodwin